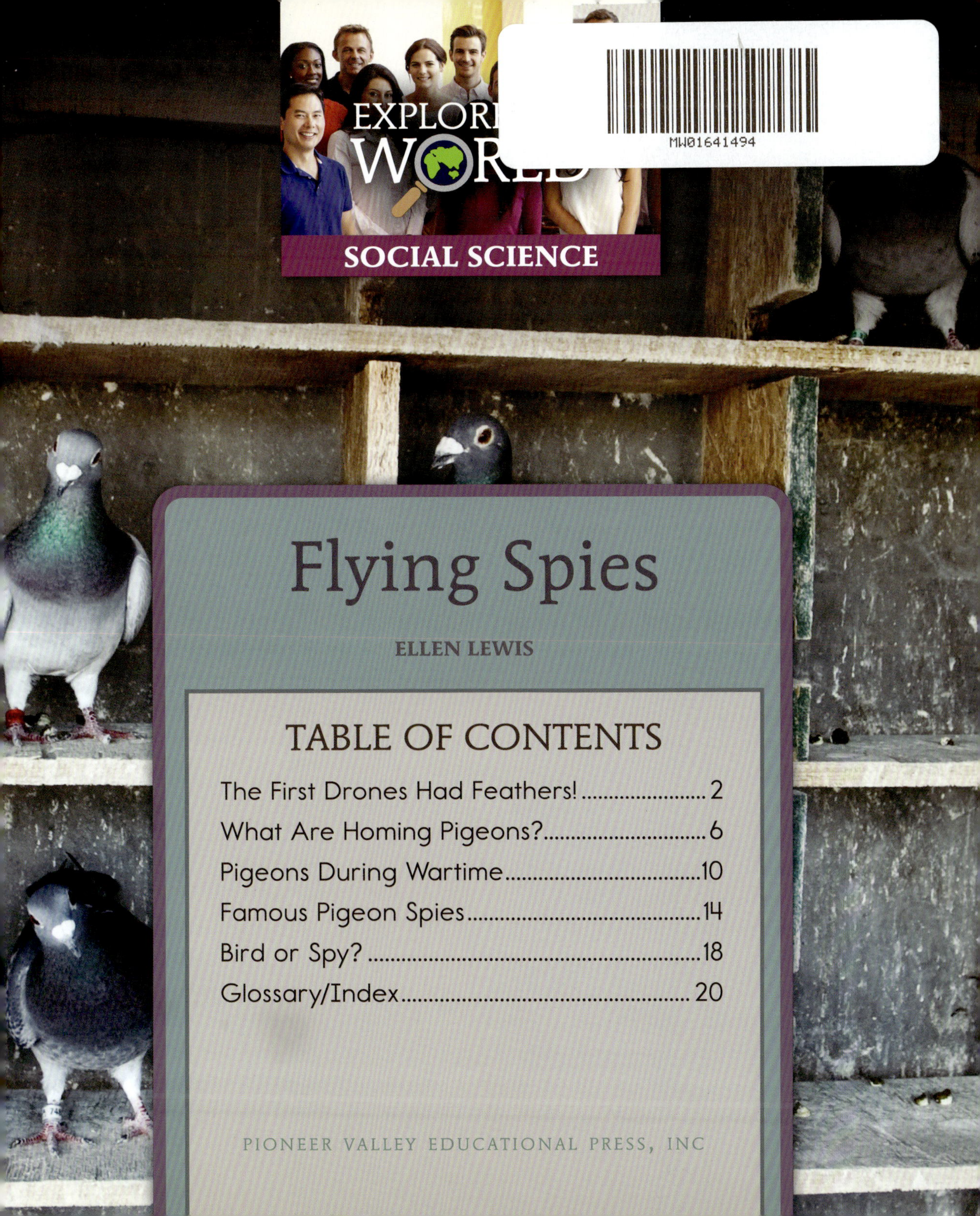

Flying Spies

ELLEN LEWIS

TABLE OF CONTENTS

PIONEER VALLEY EDUCATIONAL PRESS, INC

THE FIRST DRONES HAD FEATHERS!

A spy gathers information about someone or something. There are many kinds of spies. Some spies are human, and some are not. Did you know that robots and animals can be flying spies?

Drones are flying robots that are controlled by a person on the ground.
Drones can take pictures and deliver messages. This makes them useful for spying.

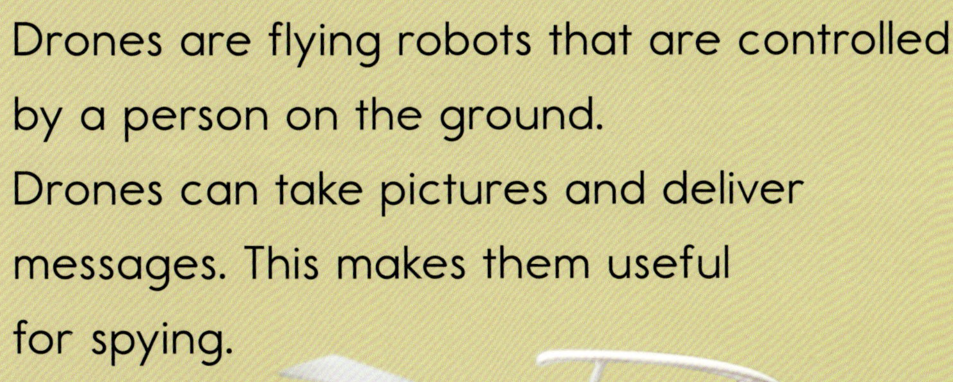

Long ago, before there were drones or cell phones, there was another kind of spy. It flew in the air like a drone, but it had feathers. It was a spy pigeon! These birds were used to collect and deliver information.

Pigeons have been **SPIES** for over 2,000 years. Spy pigeons have saved thousands of lives by delivering important messages during the world wars.

The next time you are outside at recess or at the park, look closely at the pigeons around you. Are they just pests trying to steal your sandwich crumbs? In the world of spying, all is not what it seems.

MORE TO EXPLORE

The International Spy Museum in Washington, DC, includes a whole **EXHIBIT** about spy pigeons. You can also learn more about the role of pigeons as spies by visiting the museum's website at: http://www.spymuseum.org/

WHAT ARE HOMING PIGEONS?

Some pigeons are called **homing** pigeons. This means they can find their way home from far away. Homing pigeons can be trained to carry messages written on small pieces of paper.

First, the pigeon trainer makes a home base for the bird. This is a safe place where the pigeon can find food and water. The pigeon is then taken a few miles away and let go into the air. The pigeon will fly straight back to its home. After that, the trainer will take the pigeon farther and farther away. Each time, the pigeon will find its way home. Finally, the pigeon is ready to go on a long trip, perhaps to carry secret information!

Once the pigeon has been trained, it can carry a camera, a message on its leg, or even a backpack! This does not hurt the pigeon. After it has been released by the sender, the pigeon will carry its load back home to the receiver. That can mean flying through thunderstorms, snow, or other dangerous conditions.

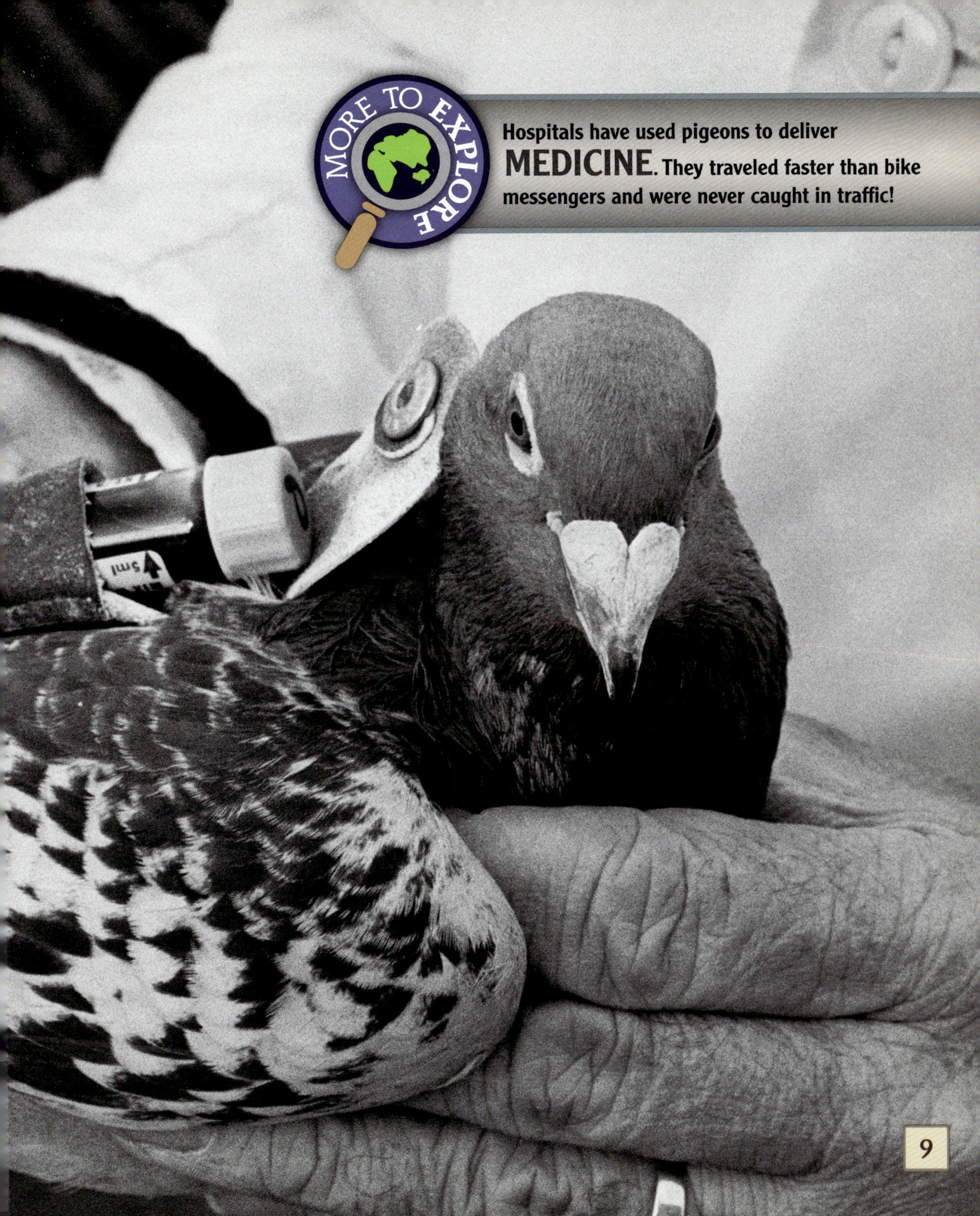
MORE TO EXPLORE
Hospitals have used pigeons to deliver
MEDICINE. They traveled faster than bike messengers and were never caught in traffic!
5ml

PIGEONS DURING WARTIME

Long ago, spy pigeons were used during wars to deliver messages. Soldiers wrote messages on small pieces of paper and hid them in little tubes. The tubes were then tied to the pigeons' legs. Some spy pigeons even wore cameras to take pictures of the enemy. The spy pigeons could fly all day and travel long distances.

Photo Credits: State Library of Victoria

Photo Credit: State Library of Victoria

At least 100,000 pigeons were used as spies in World War I. They carried messages or took pictures with small cameras strapped to their backs.

Many of the pigeons flew through gunfire to deliver their messages. Most of them delivered their messages safely, but some were hit by bullets. Pigeons were so important that you could be sent to prison for hurting one!

FAMOUS PIGEON SPIES

These brave birds risked their lives to help soldiers during war. Some pigeons became so famous that stories, books, and poems were written about them.

One famous spy pigeon was named Cher Ami, which means "Dear Friend." American soldiers were trapped by the enemy. They were surrounded. They had no food left and could not call for help. Their only hope was to have their pigeon, Cher Ami, get a message to their friends.

A soldier stuffed a note in a tube and tied it to Cher Ami's leg. During her flight, Cher Ami was shot. Somehow she was able to keep flying even though she was badly injured. Cher Ami delivered her message and 200 men were saved!

Cher Ami almost died. Doctors saved her life, but she lost one of her legs. The doctors made her a wooden leg to replace it. She was given a medal for her bravery. She became so famous that her body was **preserved** after she died. It is now on display at a museum in Washington, DC.

There was another famous pigeon spy named G.I. Joe. He lived with soldiers who had **occupied** a small town in enemy territory. No one else knew that the soldiers were hiding in the town. Their radios were broken, so they could not share information with anyone.

The American army was planning to bomb the enemy town. The soldiers' only hope was to send a message to their friends by pigeon.

G.I. Joe carried their message tied to his leg. He flew very fast and made the 20-mile trip in 20 minutes. He arrived just in time. If he had arrived five minutes later, it would have been too late!

During World War II, 32 pigeons were awarded medals.

BIRD OR SPY?

Pigeons are smart. They are **fearless**, loyal, and determined to carry out their missions. The next time you see a pigeon, look closely and think about the facts you have learned about spy pigeons. Perhaps that pigeon is a flying spy!

But, *Cher Ami*, upon my word,
You modest, modest little bird;
Now don't you know that you forgot?
Tell how your breast and leg were shot.

"Oh, yes, the day we crossed the Meuse,
I flew to Rampont with the news;
Again the bullets came like hail,
I thought for sure that I should fail.

The bullets buzzed by like a bee,
So close, it almost frightened me;
One struck the feathers of this sail,
Another went right through my tail.

But when I got back to the rear,
I found they hit me, here and here;
But that is nothing, never mind;
Old *Poilu*, there is nearly blind.

I only care for what they said,
For when they saw the way I bled,
And found in front a swollen lump,
The message hanging from this stump;

The French and Mine said, '*Tres bien,*'
Or 'Very good'—American.
'*Mon Cher Ami*, you brought good news;
Our Army's gone across the Meuse!

You surely had a lucky call'
And so I'm glad. I guess that's all.
I'll sit, so pardon me, I beg;
It's hard a-standing on one leg!"

Cher Ami

By: Harry Webb Farrington

Cher Ami, how do you do!
Listen, let me talk to you;
I'll not hurt you, don't you see?
Come a little close to me.

Little scrawny blue and white
Messenger for men who fight,
Tell me of the deep, red scar,
There, just where no feathers are.

What about your poor left leg?
Tell me, *Cher Ami*, I beg.
Boys and girls are at a loss,
How you won that Silver Cross.

"The finest fun that came to me
Was when I went with Whittlesey;
We marched so fast, so far ahead!
'We all are lost,' the keeper said;

'*Mon Cher Ami*—that's my dear friend—
You are the one we'll have to send;
The whole battalion now is lost,
And you must win at any cost.'

So with the message tied on tight;
I flew up straight with all my might,
Before I got up high enough,
Those watchfull guns began to puff.

Machine-gun bullets came like rain,
You'd think I was an aeroplane;
And when I started to the rear,
My! the shot was coming near!

But on I flew, straight as a bee;
The wind could not catch up with me,
Until I dropped out of the air,
Into our own men's camp, so there!"

GLOSSARY

exhibit

a collection of images or objects shown at a museum

fearless

not afraid; very brave

homing

knowing how to return back to a starting point

occupied

having taken over a place

preserved

something that is kept from rotting

INDEX